A IS FOR AFRIKA,
S IS FOR SOVEREIGNTY

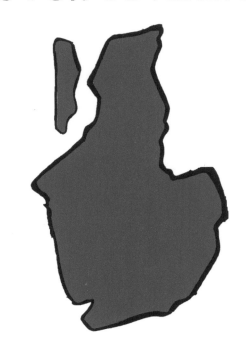

Baoku Duduyemi
Illustrated by Saleam Bey
Foreword by Marimba Ani

Kibolebole Educational Institute
Atlanta, GA

ISBN: 978-1-7321617-0-2

First Edition

Library of Congress Control Number: 2018952525

Published by:

Kibolebole Educational Institute
964 Ralph David Abernathy Blvd SW
Suite C
Box 5
Atlanta, GA 30310

www.kibolebole.com

To our Ancestors, and every Afrikan returned to heal the wounds of oppression.

To my wife, Evelyn, and every Afrikan directing the education and socialization of an Afrikan child.

To my children, Ayodele and Aperin, and every Afrikan child learning to serve Afrikan people.

To every Afrikan who ever has, or ever will, challenge oppression.

Your victories will be celebrated.

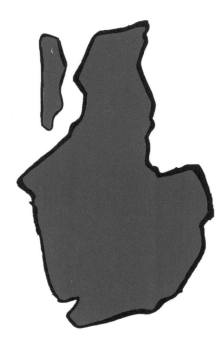

Acknowledgments

Medaase Pa to the ancestors for all that you have given me. Your work is the foundation of this work.

Medaase Pa to my son, Aperin, for inspiring this work. Medaase Pa to my wife, Evelyn, and my daughter, Ayodele, for trusting me with this work. I appreciate your encouragement, permission, sacrifice, and support.

Medaase Pa to Nana Marimba Ani and the Afrikan Heritage After School Program (AHAP) for introducing me to many of the concepts found in this book. The greatest aspirations of your work are the greatest aspirations of this work.

Medaase Pa to Ena Afiya and Agya Wekesa Madzimoyo and AYA Educational Institute (AYA) for guiding me in fighting, healing, and building with our people. The theme of your work is the theme of this work.

Medaase Pa to those who edited or otherwise contributed to this work, including: Nana Marimba Ani, Ena Afiya and Agya Wekesa Madzimoyo, Evelyn Duduyemi, Ena Yaa and Mwalimu K. Bomani Baruti, Professor Terry Benton, Baba Basir M'Chawi, and Uriah Yisrael.

Medaase Pa to Mwalimu K. Bomani Baruti for your book, Sesh. Medaase Pa to Angela Freeman and Dawud Anyabwile for your consulting. Your guidance contributed greatly to the completion and publishing of this work.

Medaase Pa to Saleam Bey for your healing illustrations. Medaase Pa to Tenechia Stokley for selecting such wonderful colors.

Medaase Pa to Sister Africa Starchia for creating the illustration used to advertise and raise funds for this work. Medaase Pa to Iya Adeniji Lawrence, Anthony Simmons, Nilajah Maat, Aunkh Aakhu, and Akua Abofari for financing this work.

If I have forgotten to acknowledge anyone, please forgive me. I appreciate your support. This work was possible because of your efforts and your trust.

Foreword by Nana Marimba Ani

This book is wonderful! Baoku Duduyemi has done what I have always wanted to do. He has created a "primer" of Afrikan Consciousness. A is for Afrika, S is for Sovereignty is an introduction to Aduno So, the Afrikan World View. It is serious, yet playful. As Afrikan parents and grandparents read this text to their children, they, along with their children, become immersed in a discussion and explanation of Afrikan Deep Thought. It is compelling and inviting, as the readers and listeners move through an alphabet of Afrikan concepts. The book is Afrikan Child-centered. It is easily understandable, yet intellectually challenging, encouraging spiritual and ideological growth. A is for Afrika, S is for Sovereignty can be a catalyst for the development of Suban Pa, "good character." It offers lessons that enumerate and affirm Afrikan cultural values and codes of conduct and behavior. It is filled with information concerning Afrikan life, ourstory ("history"), and civilization.

Baoku Duduyemi has created a carefully prepared, clearly stated, beautifully presented, well-written, and well-researched book for Afrikan families to experience together. As young children participate in this experience, their vocabulary expands, they learn to read, and the seeds of an Afrikan Sovereign Consciousness are planted. Brother Baoku is a gifted writer who uses his talents to touch the spirit of very young Afrikan children. The book is filled with such gems and brilliant images as "Grandpa wraps me in stories," and "as I munch on my music and make meals of the sun."

Nana Baffour Amankwatia (Baba Asa Hilliard) advised us to focus on the "mass socialization" of our children. Baoku Duduyemi has produced a formidable weapon; a tool for the first stage of Afrikan warrior training. This book must serve as a model for others. We need an arsenal of primers such as this which together will constitute the "frontline" of our project to build an Afrikan Sovereign World Order.

A is for Afrika
Where my ancestors roam
Some call it Alkebulan
I call it home
My Asili was born there
And I'll return one day
So let's hear it for Afrika
Abibifahodie!

B is for Baba
He always buys Black
He's building a business
Bakes cookies in fact
With Mama he's balanced
Not a king or a chief
He gets help when he needs it
And in us has belief

C is for culture
Good character too
Caught and taught
From our Nanas
To me and to you
It protects and connects us
Wherever we live
So I'll use my Black power
For the whole collective

D is for drums
That I play with my hands
Djembes and Dun Duns
Daddy's pots
And some pans
I'm finding the rhythm
Black magic's in me
I'll dance and I'll sing
Claim our destiny

E is for Elders
They earned their position
Educate and advise
Even when we don't listen
Experienced in emotions,
Economics, and such
And will still rub my tummy
When I've eaten too much

F is for family and all my Black friends
We have fun while we're learning,
Fight oppression, and win
I can share all my feelings
Get support and far more
Because that's what my family and friends are all for

G is for greeting like most Afrikans do
Is your family well?
And your grandparents too?
Is your garden still growing?
Does your health seem all right?
Glad to hear it
Great to see you
Give thanks and good night

H is for happy
My favorite feeling
When I do my best work
Or a hurt begins healing
When crocheting a hat
Or while climbing a tree
Or helping at home
'Cause my family needs me

I is for insight
And imagination
When I build with my blocks
I can "image a nation"
I trust my intelligence
And my intuition
Pay attention when Mommy
Instructs me to listen

J is for Jegnoch
Champions for our race
Our culture, our justice, our people, our place
I feel joy when they teach me
To do what they do
So I can join in their work
Loving Afrikans too

K is for Kala
A new rising sun
One Kanda connected
A nation begun
An ancestor returned
To keep Promises made
I'll build Kujitawala
Get support when afraid

L is for language
The face of our way
So I'm learning an Afrikan
language today
The rhythm and tones
Sound to me like a song
So I listen, take lessons,
Then talk all day long

M is for Melanin
The blackness in me
Links me to emotions
Helps my memory
It protects, and connects me,
And helps me have fun
As I munch on my music
And make meals of the sun

N is for nation
Ask Umi and Abba
They shout, "Free the land!"
Use Nguzo Saba
They know every principle
Call each by name
Now I'm learning them too
And our Nia's the same

O is for organizing,
Opposing oppression
Overthrowing destroyers
Obsessed with aggression
I observe as my parents
Plan, gather, and fight
I dream of our winning
Overjoyed by our might

P is for power
Black people's connection
The traditions we learn
Our culture's protection
I remember that words
Can both heal and destroy
I use mine for Black power
Black peace and Black joy

Q is for quilt
With patterns,
Connections
Symbols and knots,
Messages,
Directions
Grandma helps me choose fabric
Cut pieces and sew
Grandpa wraps me in stories
From my head to my toe

R is for rhythm
Giving
Receiving
Rising and setting
Resisting
Retreating
Whether I'm jumping rope
Or dancing to drums
I find rhythm in play
And in work to be done

S is for sovereignty
Afrikan self-reliance
Sustained by Black power
And Afrikan science
I'll sow seeds and sew clothing
At home and at school
Strategize with my family
How to maintain self-rule

T is for trust
In myself and in you
Our teachings, technologies,
Our truths and world view
From Afrikan culture
Come values and rules
When it's my turn to build
I'll use Afrikan tools

U is for Ujamaa
"Familyhood"
And Ubuntu
Like umuntu ngumuntu ngabantu in Zulu
"A person is a person because of people"
You see
I'll hold up my community
The way it holds up me

V is for victory
A Pan-Afrikan vision
Of nation, world order,
And authentic decision
Seeing with my heart
Hearing *So Dayi*
I'll use Afrikan power
To write our destiny

W is for will
To build a sovereign Black nation
With Afrikan wisdom
Self-determination
I'll learn stories of warriors
From my family tree
Keep fighting, keep winning,
And remember they're me

X is for (ex)ercise
We know you're confused
That does not start with X
Mom and Dad aren't amused
We know it's important
To run, jump, and play,
And carrying that big
Xylophone
Would just get in the way

Y is for youth
In every generation
Preparing to manage our Afrikan nation
Using yesterday's lessons
And every success
I will learn what I'm taught
And show my Grandma my best

Z is for Zodiac
The path of our sun
Afrikan science and culture
Rolled up into one
Afrikan constellations
We can use to track time
I'll find all 43
And for my favorite yell, "mine!"

Glossary

Abba   Abba means father in several Afrikan languages, including Afaan Oromo and Afar. It is also written as Aaba, Aba, and Abbaa.

Asili   Nana Marimba Ani uses Asili (KiSwahili for seed) as "The seed of a culture."

Abibifahodie   Abibifahodie means Afrikan liberation in Asante Twi.

Baba   Baba means father in several Afrikan languages, including chiShona and Yoruba.

Constellation   A constellation is a set of stars that appear to be located close together in the sky, and form a picture when we imagine lines connecting them. Afrikan people use these pictures to travel, measure time, grow food, and tell our sacred stories.

Culture   Culture is all of the things that we create together, as a Race, to make life good for us. Culture connects us to each other. Our Ancestors created languages, science, math, music, art, ways of teaching and learning, and ways of relating to each other through this connection. They created the first "families" and the first "societies." They put all of these things together to form a way of life. Culture is everything that our Ancestors built together into "Afrikan civilization." Nana Marimba Ani says that Afrikan Culture acts like an "Immune System" for Afrikan people.

Insight   Insight is the meaning we give to facts, and the understanding we gain about how something works when we ask ourselves, "Is it good for Afrikan people?"

Intuition   Intuition is the understanding that comes when Afrikan people combine their thoughts with their feelings. Our intuition is expanded through the experiences of Afrikan people, past and present. It is our inner voice, our Afrikan ancestral wisdom, our intelligence of the heart.

Jegnoch   Jegnoch means "heroes" or "brave ones" (in Amharic). It is the plural form of Jegna. Jegnoch are brave Afrikan warriors who love Afrikan people. They protect our people, our land, and our culture. Jegnoch are skilled and dependable Afrikans. They guide us in fighting, healing, and building for Afrikan people. Jegnoch trust themselves, our people, and our way.

Kala sun   Kala is the Black sun of birth and rebirth in Bakongo cosmology. Tata Kimbwandènde Kia Bunseki Fu-Kiau explains that Kala sun rises toward the mastery of life.

Kanda   Kanda is a Kikongo word for a community of biologically related members. Nana Marimba Ani uses Kanda to describe Race as a family, and as the largest community with members related through blood.

Kujitawala   Kujitawala means self-governance or self-rule in Kiswahili.

Melanin   Melanin is a special substance found in Afrikan people and in nature that does many wonderful things, like taking in different types of energy and using that energy as food to keep our bodies working at their best. Melanin connects Afrikan people to everything.

Muntu   Muntu means human being or person in Bantu languages. (Bantu is the plural form of Muntu.)

Nanas   Nanas are grandmothers or elder women. It is also written as Nannas.

Nia   Nia means purpose in Kiswahili, and is the fifth principle of the Nguzo Saba.

Nguzo Saba   Nguzo Saba means Seven Principles in Kiswahili. It is the Afrikan value system introduced and reinforced through Kwanzaa[1].

Oppression   Oppression includes all the ways that a Race of people are attacked and made to do things that are not their way. Nana Marimba Ani calls the historic and ongoing oppression of Afrikan people the "Maafa."

So Dayi   So Dayi means "Clear Word" in Dogona. Nana Marimba Ani describes So Dayi as "Vision"—hearing the collective experiences of Afrikan people, past and present, and using our imagination to build an "Afrikan" future.

Sovereignty   Afrikan Sovereignty is the power to protect, defend, and advance the collective interests of Afrikan people. It is the power to regain and preserve Afrikan nationhood. It is the power to enforce and reinforce Afrikan values and laws without interference. Sovereignty is absolute Afrikan power, and it supports the survival and growth of Afrikan people.

Ubuntu   Ubuntu is the Afrikan process of humanness in several Nguni Bantu languages. A few of these languages are isiNedeble, isiXhosa, isiZulu, and siSwati.

Umi   Umi is a mother, grandmother, or elder woman.

World View   World view is the way people think as a Race. Our Afrikan world view is based on Afrikan Culture. It gives us basic definitions, such as what it means to be "human," what it means to "live," what Nature is, what it means to be an Ancestor, and many more important things.

---

1   Kwanzaa is a Pan-Afrikan celebration of Afrikan culture. Both the Nguzo Saba and Kwanzaa were popularized through the efforts of several individuals and organizations, including the Us Organization, the Congress of Afrikan People (CAP), the EAST Educational and Cultural Center for People of African Descent, the Institute for Positive Education (IPA), and the Committee for Unified Newark (CFUN).

Author's Note

Many of you now know me through this work. Others recognize me as "the cookie man." As the cookie man, I make delicious vegan cookies that support Afrikan people. I once baked Afrika-shaped chocolate sugar cookies that were so delicious that after biting into one, a brother shook his head and yelled (in a very crowded coffee house), "Man, this is a good cookie!" Hearing this, another brother, Ebrima, stood up, raised his arms, and shouted, "Of course they're good! It's Afrika!"

This thought, this feeling, this love for Afrika, is what I work to inspire in my family and in our people. With that in mind, I wrote *A is for Afrika, S is for Sovereignty* for Afrikan children and adults—rhyming poems, warm, bright colors, and content that serves Afrikan people. Mwalimu K. Bomani Baruti described it as ". . . one of those books which will make frontline parenting so much easier . . .," and given the increased active aggression against Afrikan people, guiding Afrikan children along a path that serves Afrikan people has become increasingly important.

I structured *A is for Afrika, S is for Sovereignty* so that both children and adults can heal and succeed together—guided by a resource written intentionally with the parent-child interaction in mind. Like many picture books, *A is for Afrika, S is for Sovereignty* is designed to be read aloud, allowing the reader to support the child's understanding of the deep concepts and symbolic illustrations. While it's widely known that reading vocabulary-rich picture books aloud supports children in developing a rich vocabulary, this elder-approved work was designed to develop a rich Afrikan-centered vocabulary. Some use the written word for the purpose of establishing authority. We are using the written word to heal the wounds of oppression and inspire your story.

I relearned a number of lessons while creating *A is for Afrika, S is for Sovereignty*—some about the impact of oppression on our people, and some about its impact on me. When an elder suggested an addition to the glossary and followed my quizzical look with instructions to "get more connected," I responded by reconnecting to my family, our people, our wounds, and our way. I'm still reconnecting, and I invite you to do the same.

A is for Afrika, S is for Sovereignty does not stand alone. It is supported by Afrikan-centered courses, lectures, and a skill set that, when used together and applied to the text, generate better results for both the parent and child academically, emotionally, and socially. To inquire how to participate in these offerings and try on the skill set, please contact me at info@kibolebole.com. You may also visit our website at www.kibolebole.com.

Abibifahodie!

Baoku Duduyemi, AYA WHB Facilitator

CPSIA information can be obtained
at www.ICGtesting.com
Printed in the USA
BVHW062152061220
594506BV00001BA/3